STITCHES IN TIME TRAVEL

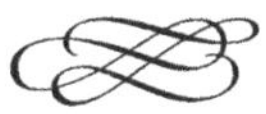

PETER G. REYNOLDS

This book is dedicated to the four most important people in my life: my wife, my best friend, my accountant and my muse.

Lucky for me they're all the same person, which really saves on birthday and Christmas cards.

CHAPTER 1

THE TRAP

It's hard being an only child when you have siblings.

This was particularly true at Christmas. Charlotte longed for the days when she was the centre of attention and the tree was surrounded with gifts just for her. Now she had to share the spotlight with her four-year-old sister, Beatrix. It wasn't fair, but then a lot of things hadn't been fair lately.

Charlotte shivered. At this time of year, and this late at night, the cobblestone floor in the old manor house was cold even when wearing shoes. Charlotte was barefoot. The cold stung her feet with every step, but the rumbling in her tummy would not be denied. She should have worn her slippers. *Mother* was always scolding her for not wearing her slippers. But then *Mother* was always scolding her for something. *I hate her*, thought Charlotte, wishing she were staying with her Mom this Christmas – where the weather was warm, and there was no need for slippers. But this was *Mother's* year, and that was that.

Christmas with Mother meant being shipped off to her Nana's. Her Mother's mother. Not to be confused with Gran, her Mom's mom. Of course, having two moms wasn't confusing to Charlotte, but she'd given up explaining it to her friends.

The cookie jar was almost within reach. It was on the top shelf, surrounded by cured meats, dried fruits and smelly cheeses. A mouse ran over Charlotte's foot, and she stifled a scream. Luckily, or perhaps unluckily, mice were common at Nana's, so Charlotte wasn't too surprised. The tiny visitor scurried across the pantry floor with a large crumb of rye bread in its mouth and pushed itself into a sagging bag of flour, which had a convenient hole in the bottom.

"Is that you Charlotte?" rang a too familiar voice from the other room.

Charlotte froze. She'd been avoiding that voice all day. This year Nana was obsessed with the family's Christmas quilt and had been pestering Charlotte to work on it. Charlotte had managed to avoid doing it since she arrived, but it was Christmas Eve and she was running out of excuses.

"Come here, Charlotte, I have something for you."

It's a trap, thought Charlotte. *Lull you in with the promise of a sweet, only to be trapped into another unending story that always begins with when-I-was-a-girl-not-much older-than-you.*

"Charlotte?" repeated Nana. "Come out of the pantry."

Charlotte sighed. "Yes, Nana. Coming."

The *great room*, as her Nana called it, was grossly mislabelled in Charlotte's opinion. It was *large*, to be sure, with a fireplace big enough to stand in, but it was hardly great. The tapestries hanging from the walls were moth-eaten and faded. The crown mouldings around the ceiling were cracked and, in some places, missing entirely. The walls and ceiling were stained black from smoke above the hearth. Even the windows, once beautiful stained glass, were now either broken or crusted with dirt.

The only thing that could be called *great* was the Christmas tree. Nearly touching the ceiling, it was covered in handmade ornaments made by past generations of children, and more recently, by Charlotte and her sister Beatrix. It was wrapped with garlands of popcorn and dried cranberries. Charlotte had heard stories that the family used to decorate the tree with candles, but now it was lit with twinkling electric lights. *Much more sensible*, thought Charlotte.

In the middle of the room, in an old chair, sat Nana. She was ancient, *probably at least fifty*, thought Charlotte. She had bright, expressive eyes and wore a simple, white cotton nightgown, embroidered with lilies on the sleeves. Nana loved lilies. Charlotte vaguely remembered lilies had something to do with the patron saint of families. Her Nana had been raised by nuns after the war and her family meant everything to her.

Beside Nana, on a fragile-looking table, sat a steaming mug of tea. Charlotte had noticed on previous visits that Nana would leave her tea there to cool each evening, only to forget about it and drink it cold. It had become a private family joke.

Nana patted her lap. "Charlotte. Come sit here."

Charlotte approached. The ragged carpet was a welcome relief from the cold cobblestones. She was getting a little old to be sitting on laps, but she agreed without protest.

"Are you cold?" Nana asked.

"Yes. Beatrix took all the covers." *She takes everything,* thought Charlotte.

"Don't be so hard on your sister," said Nana gently, reading Charlotte's mind.

Charlotte rolled her eyes. *Of course you'd take her side. She's named after you.*

"I hear cookies help when you're cold. Can I have one of yours, dear?"

"Uh, sure," replied Charlotte sheepishly. She dug two stolen madeleines out of the pocket of her robe and handed one to Nana, who broke it down the middle, placing half in a small, faded blue handkerchief. *For later*, she would always say. She then folded the handkerchief and put it in Charlotte's pocket. The two then sat in silence for a minute or two, slowly savouring their guilty treat.

"I'm so glad you're up. It's not too late."

"Too late for what?

"To tell you a story from when I was a girl."

The trap! thought Charlotte. *I've fallen for it again!*

Nana lifted up a thick, patchwork blanket tucked between her chair and the table. "Every girl in our family, when she's ten years old, adds her story to our family quilt on Christmas Eve."

Nana unfolded the quilt. Each square was unique. Some were embroidered with words and images, while others were sewn with buttons or beads. There was no pattern to the squares, but Charlotte saw beauty in all that chaos. It was her family's history – their passions and dreams, all lovingly stitched into a physical memory that you could literally wrap yourself in.

Nana pointed to a portrait on the wall of a wild-looking woman. Her smile was too big for her face, and she had a stick of cinnamon protruding from her hair. "My mother, your great-grandmother, Mary-Charlotte Gladstone, knew the importance of family traditions."

At that point, Charlotte tuned her grandmother out. She knew this story all too well, but Nana always repeated it as if she'd never heard it before. Mary-Charlotte Gladstone, the matriarch of the family. The wild one, who had trapped beavers in Canada, travelled by herself to India and was an avid balloonist. The woman Charlotte was named after but could never live up to.

Charlotte ran her hand across the quilt lightly, taking in every stitch. "It's *okay*," she said finally, knowing any level of enthusiasm only made Nana's stories last longer. Questions did, too, but one slipped out before Charlotte could catch it. "Why haven't I seen it before?"

"You have," replied Nana, ignoring Charlotte's well-practiced apathy. "It normally hangs in the dining hall. Been there since I was a child."

That explains it, thought Charlotte. *The old dining hall was even colder than the pantry. Nana didn't even bother heating it anymore.*

Another question slipped out. "Why when we're ten?"

"What's that, dear?" replied Nana. Her hearing was not what it once was.

"Why do the girls in our family add to the quilt when they're ten?" Charlotte repeated.

"Oh," said Nana. "Because that's how old our Christmas Angel is." As if that was all the answer anyone needed.

Charlotte looked incredulously at her. "Our Christmas Angel?"

"Of course, dear. She visits each daughter of the household on their tenth Christmas Eve."

Despite herself, this sparked Charlotte's curiosity. "Did she visit Mother?"

"You'll have to ask her. The Christmas Angel only stays until the last stroke of midnight, but she always brings a gift."

"What did she give you?" asked Charlotte.

Nana looked away as if savouring the memory. "Hope," she said finally, popping the last bite of cookie in her mouth and chewing it between her few remaining teeth.

Christmas Angels? Christmas quilts? Charlotte couldn't get out of there fast enough. She hopped off Nana's knee and headed for the stairs.

"Wait," said Nana. "It's not too late. We can work on the quilt together."

"Thanks, Nana, but I'm pretty tired," replied Charlotte, stretching her arms above her head and yawning in an exaggerated fashion.

"But if you don't complete your patch, the Christmas Angel won't visit," Nana warned.

"That's OK," said Charlotte dismissively.

Nana looked disappointed, and Charlotte felt a pang of guilt. She walked over and kissed Nana on the cheek and headed out of the great room.

"Charlotte," said Nana, holding out the quilt. "To keep you warm."

Charlotte thanked her as she took the quilt and hurried up to her room. Her feet were still cold, but the thought of cuddling under the thick quilt warmed her. It was so big she had to hold it above her head, and even then, it trailed on the floor, threatening to trip her. She walked carefully and eventually made it to her room. Inside, her unwanted sister dominated half of their large bed, wholly cocooned in pillows and bed sheets, leaving the other half cold and desolate. Charlotte threw the quilt onto the bed, grabbed a small flashlight from her nightstand, and then climbed in herself.

CHAPTER 2

A SEA OF COTTON

The moon was full this Christmas Eve, illuminating the bedroom in a soft, dream-like light. Charlotte flipped the quilt over and dove under it, not even bothering to remove her robe. Lying on her back, the quilt completely covering her, she held it up with her arms and legs, creating a makeshift tent. Turning on her flashlight, Charlotte could see the images and stories sewn into it. *Memories of Christmases past,* she breathed, tracing her hand over the different patches.

Charlotte had to admit the women in her mother's family were talented. Each patch was wonderfully detailed. Her great-grandmother's was a colourful map of the world, showing all the exotic places she wanted to visit. It was intricately stitched with seashells and silks of silver and gold. Charlotte found herself mesmerized by it.

Slowly, Charlotte began to crawl on her back towards the foot of the bed. She followed the memories of her family going back generations – everyday scenes of ice skating and tobogganing to fantastical images of unicorns and handsome princes. Then, beneath the patch of a young girl sitting on a galloping horse, she paused. *The quilt can't be this big*, she thought, and she reached her arms out to grab the edges. Only her hands didn't find the edges, just more fabric.

Charlotte tried to throw the quilt off her, but for some reason it was now too heavy. Charlotte then turned on her stomach and crawled towards where she knew the foot of the bed was, but all she found was a sea of cotton. "I must be dreaming," she said aloud, as if naming it would rob the dream of its power. She closed her eyes tightly, crawling faster, but when she opened them again, the quilt was still there.

This is just a dream, Charlotte told herself again and again, believing it less and less as time passed. Her crawling seemed to last hours and she had long ago given up on what direction she was crawling in. She was sure she'd find her way out, until she didn't. Sure she would wake up, until she didn't. Sure this nightmare would end. Until it didn't.

Eventually, she collapsed from exhaustion, the soft bed sheets absorbing her tears. There was no way out, no escape from this nightmare.

And then she heard singing.

It was very faint, but in the heavy silence under the quilt, the music was a beacon of hope. Holding her flashlight in one hand, Charlotte crawled as fast as she could towards the sound. She was almost able to make out the words when she tumbled out of bed and onto the hardwood floor.

Charlotte slowly stood up, any discomfort from the fall masked by embarrassment. *I was dreaming,* she chided herself, feeling silly for being so frightened just moments earlier. She looked over at the bed to see if she'd woken Beatrix, but she wasn't there. *Probably crawled in with Nana*, thought Charlotte, looking at the door that connected their rooms.

Her eyes adjusting to the moonlight, Charlotte could see the bedroom was *different*. Even in the dim light, the bed looked new. The brass knobs on the bedposts were shiny, not the tarnished green she remembered. The walls and ceiling were clean and white without a hint of peeling and Charlotte swore she could smell fresh paint. Even the curtains were different; luxurious purple drapes with gold tassels hung from floor to ceiling. Charlotte walked over and looked behind them. The windows were new as well, though the glass was wavier than she recalled.

The singing was coming from outside, just below her window. It was a chorus of voices, adults and children. *Carolers?* thought Charlotte. *Who does that anymore?*

"Very funny," she said aloud. Clearly, someone was playing a joke on her. Beatrix loved to play little pranks, though she'd have needed a lot of help to pull off something like this.

Charlotte looked under the bed. "Bea?" She looked behind the curtains. "Bea? OK. You got me."

Nothing. *Maybe they didn't think I'd wake until morning?* Her slippers were also missing, another little joke. Barefoot once again, she dropped her flashlight into the pocket of her robe and walked to the door leading to the hallway, confident she wouldn't be able to sleep until this mystery was solved.

Opening the door, she immediately had to shield her eyes. The hallway lights were bright. Peeking through her fingers, Charlotte stared in disbelief at flames dancing behind tulip-shaped sconces. Gas lights? *What's going on?*

Suddenly a man walked past Charlotte, making her jump. He was dressed very formally in black pants and a long black jacket. Charlotte would have screamed if her first thought wasn't that he looked exactly like a penguin. He turned and nodded respectfully to Charlotte, uttering "Miss" as he passed. He was obviously in a hurry. Charlotte followed him just in time to see him disappear behind the wall to the servants' stairs.

In the past, Charlotte had been told, servants weren't supposed to be seen. Nana's house was riddled with secret stairs and corridors and they were the areas of the old manor house Charlotte most enjoyed exploring. She'd even used them to spy on her moms one year, hearing them argue about silly things adults argue about.

Hands shaking, Charlotte slowly pushed on the part of the wall where she knew the secret door was. It opened much more smoothly than she remembered, barely making a sound. Inside was dark, lit only by a single, simple wall sconce in the middle of the stairway leading down. Charlotte was familiar with these stairs and, in truth, wouldn't have needed the light at all. She quickly descended, any fear forgotten in the face of such a mystery.

At the bottom of the stairs, Charlotte peered into the familiar pantry, which was no longer familiar. Inside was a flurry of activity. The penguin was nowhere to be seen, but several women wearing long grey dresses and white aprons were buzzing about, gathering meat, cheese and spices and taking them out to the kitchen beyond. If they noticed Charlotte, they didn't say anything. It was as if she was invisible to them.

A girl about Charlotte's age walked into the pantry. She wore a beautiful if uncomfortable looking dress. It was brightly patterned and wide at the bottom. Her feet were hidden as she walked, making it look like she glided across the floor. She clutched a small piece of cloth.

All the women in the room immediately stopped what they were doing. They turned to the girl and curtsied. "How can we help you, milady?" one of them said.

"I want a raspberry tart," the girl responded. It didn't seem like a request.

"I'm sorry, Miss," replied one of the older women. "Your mother gave us strict instructions. No sweets before dinner."

"I want a raspberry tart!" the girl repeated, stamping her foot for emphasis. Charlotte was sure *that* wasn't a request.

"No, Miss," said the older woman. Charlotte admired her bravery. The word "no" was clearly not something this girl was used to hearing.

The little girl stood there for what seemed like an eternity, and an uncomfortable silence grew. Then, as abruptly as she entered, she turned in one fluid motion and left.

"She's a little terror," said one of the less brave women, who'd been silent up to this point.

"She's definitely an odd duckling," said another.

"Hold your tongue," scolded the older woman. "She may be demanding, but she's still our lady and deserves our respect."

"Yes, ma'am. Sorry, ma'am," the women said in unison.

The three women left the pantry without another word, carrying eggs and a variety of vegetables. Charlotte stood up, the delicious smells from the kitchen coaxing her out of her hiding spot. She didn't realize how famished she really was. A couple of madeleines hadn't nearly been enough and breakfast was still hours away. Cautiously, she approached one of the shelves that was piled high with all kinds of baked goods including biscuits, shortbread, meringues, miniature cakes and gingerbread. Charlotte reached up to take a particularly yummy looking pastry.

"Who are you?" asked a sharp voice from behind.

Charlotte felt her heart leap in her chest.

She stumbled back and crashed into one of the shelves, tearing her robe and knocking the contents on top of her. Charlotte coughed as her head was covered in flour, cinnamon sticks and other colourful spices. She wiped her eyes as best she could and saw the demanding little girl looking down at her, laughing.

Charlotte began to laugh as well. If this was a prank, it was the most elaborate one ever, and if it was a dream, it was turning out to be one of the most memorable she'd ever had.

"What's all this then?" said a very stern woman who appeared suddenly in the entrance to the pantry. She held a huge rolling pin and towered over the two girls. Her apron was covered in flour and stained with raspberry jam – at least Charlotte hoped it was raspberry jam.

"Both of you, out, out, out!" she said without waiting for a reply.

The girls looked at each other and quickly decided this woman would not take kindly to arguing. Giggling, they raced out of the pantry and Charlotte could feel the breeze from a barely missed swat go through her hair as she passed. They ran through the kitchen, which confirmed what Charlotte had been smelling. Honeyed ham, beef and something Charlotte was pretty sure was a roasted goose were resting on a long wooden table. Minced pies and Yorkshire puddings were being taken out of two ovens, neither of which Charlotte ever recalled being used. Potatoes were being mashed, cranberries boiled. It was a feast fit for a queen.

Charlotte followed the other girl out of the kitchen and down the hall. Considering what she was wearing, she was very fast. They passed through the great room and Charlotte could see that this time it was indeed great. The tapestries were vibrant, their embroidery richly detailed. The crown moulding was pristine without even a hint of a crack. The windows were beautiful stained glass and Charlotte could only imagine what they must look like during the day. Her great-grandmother's portrait had been replaced by a picture of a serious-looking Queen Victoria, whose eyes seemed to follow Charlotte as she moved. The one familiar thing was the Christmas tree, which still towered in the centre of the room – except this one was lit with candles, the lights flickering ever so slightly from an unseen breeze.

"Come on!" said Charlotte's accomplice, pulling her from the great room and down the hall. Charlotte reluctantly obeyed. Everywhere was activity, with men and women busily getting the house ready for some extravagant holiday party. They cut through the usually cold dining hall, which now was almost as busy as the kitchen. Scores of servants were setting the table with china plates, crystal glasses and elegant silverware in what could only be described as a well-choreographed dance. No one paid the girls any attention as they dodged between the dancers and headed up the stairs. Charlotte was quite out of breath by the time they reached Nana's room.

But this was not her Nana's room, at least not the one Charlotte remembered. It was ornately decorated, with a warm glow coming from the fireplace. It was also filled with porcelain dolls, each one different. *They're beautiful but a little creepy*, thought Charlotte. *All those eyes staring at you.*

The dolls' owner then kicked off her shoes and grabbed the hem of her dress, motioning Charlotte to help. The next several minutes were an education, both in fashion and, presumably, ancient torture techniques. There were five heavy layers of clothing, including one with a complex network of strings Charlotte could only assume was designed to restrict breathing.

Again, she marvelled at how fast the girl had run in this armour.

The girl grabbed a silk robe hanging from a hook nearby and put it on in one swift movement. She then pulled Charlotte onto her bed and, sitting cross-legged in front of her, held both her hands.

"Now, tell me who you are. You look a fright, but I'm sure you have a great story to tell."

"I'm Charlotte." She was too exhausted from recent efforts to say anything more.

"That's silly. *I'm* Charlotte," said the girl, looking a little disappointed.

"No, *I'm* Charlotte," repeated Charlotte more forcefully. This might be the most confusing dream she'd ever had, but if she was sure of one thing, it was her name. "Who are you?"

This question seemed to throw off the girl, who looked at Charlotte incredulously, studying her face for a hint of sarcasm.

"I'm *Mary-Charlotte Gladstone*," she answered finally. "This is my roof you're under. My bed you're sitting on. My flour you're covered in. I'm the lady of Gladstone Manor."

This time it was Charlotte's turn to look incredulous. She stared open-mouthed at the girl who was (would be?) her great-grandmother.

Mary-Charlotte seemed to take her silence for idiocy, her expression suddenly turning from irritation to pity. "Don't worry," she said gently. "You can be Charlotte, too." Leaning in closer, she added, "Can I tell you a secret?" Charlotte nodded.

Mary-Charlotte spread her arms wide. "Do you like my dolls?"

Charlotte felt little need to lie inside a dream, so she told the truth. "No. They're creepy."

Mary-Charlotte beamed. "That's exactly what I think. Oh, Second Charlotte, I just know we're going to be the best of friends."

Charlotte's new best friend then hopped off the bed and disappeared underneath it. She reappeared moments later holding two strange-looking toys.

"Daddy buys me dolls because he thinks that's what daddies do. He even buys me matching dresses so I look like my dolls."

Charlotte noted that she had indeed been dressed like one of these dolls just moments ago.

Mary-Charlotte's voice grew quiet. "My secret is ... I don't really like dolls. These are my favourites."

Mary-Charlotte handed one of the toys to Charlotte, a carousel made out of tin. Little boys and girls riding elephants, zebras and lions. They were all suspended from the roof of the carousel by monkeys holding thin coiled wires. It was festively painted and looked brand new.

"Now watch this," said Mary-Charlotte excitedly. She took a small key off her nightstand, inserted it into the base of the carousel and turned it several times.

Even though Charlotte knew what was going to happen, it didn't dampen her delight at seeing the carousel begin to turn. Mary-Charlotte's enthusiasm was infectious.

"This is called an auto-ma-ta," said Mary-Charlotte, a little too slowly for Charlotte's liking. "Uncle bought it for me in Germany. They make the most ingenious toys." She turned it over and opened up the bottom. "See, there are gears and springs inside that make everything move."

Mary-Charlotte picked up the second toy she had hidden under the bed. It looked a bit like a set of eyeglasses inside a wooden frame. Each frame held a photograph, identical as far as Charlotte could tell. She had never seen anything like it, so this time Mary-Charlotte's explanation was justified.

"It's a stereograph. Here, hold it up to your eyes using the handle."

Charlotte obliged and was rewarded with a 3-D picture of Mary-Charlotte and a tall man wearing a grey suit and a wide-brimmed hat. Both were riding camels. Behind them, a stoic looking Sphinx sat in the sand with a giant pyramid in the distance.

"It was from our big trip to Egypt last year," said Mary-Charlotte. Hardly able to contain herself. "Uncle Edward is obsessed with photography." She pointed to the two photos. "See? Each is slightly different. That's why it feels like you could reach out and touch the people in the photo. Uncle promised to show me how it works this summer when we go back to India."

The next couple of hours were an education for Charlotte, as her great-grandmother spoke about her hopes and dreams. They gushed out of her like soda from a bottle that had been shaken too violently, as if Charlotte was the first person she'd ever been able to confide in.

She wasn't like any girl Charlotte had ever met. She was insatiably curious about ... everything: science, history, math, politics. Her little pink bookshelf was stuffed with books by Jane

Austen, Mary Shelley and Lewis Carroll, but also books Charlotte couldn't begin to comprehend, including Charles Darwin's *On the Origin of Species* and the *History of Woman Suffrage, Vol 1*. It was a humbling experience. Charlotte was getting answers to questions she had never even thought to ask.

As Charlotte listened, she noticed a square of cotton sitting on Mary-Charlotte's night table. It was only partially finished but completely recognizable. It was her great-grandmother's patch from the Christmas quilt. Charlotte took it and held it gently as if it might crumble in her hands.

Mary-Charlotte looked at the patch and rolled her eyes. "Mother's making me do that."

Charlotte smiled at this. "It's wonderful."

Mary-Charlotte looked pleased at the compliment. "Did you want to help me finish it?"

Before Charlotte could answer, she was summarily pulled from the bed to a small antique desk that sat just under the bedroom window. It was a cozy spot to sit with the warmth of the fire at your back. Charlotte immediately recognized the desk. Earlier today (at least *the earlier today* that Charlotte remembered) it had sat in the foyer of Nana's house, its sole purpose a home for Nana's ancient rotary phone.

Mary-Charlotte opened the desk to reveal a large mirror and a dizzying array of drawers and compartments. Each one was filled with something different. Needles, spools of thread, seashells, buttons and seemingly endless pieces of exotic fabric.

The idea of sewing had never appealed to Charlotte. It always seemed dull. But she had to admit her great-grandmother was a good teacher and soon Charlotte was sewing like she was born to it – or at least adopted to it.

"Knot the end of your thread. Now bring the needle up through the fabric."

"Like this?"

"Yes. Now we just need to choose a fabric for—"

"How about this one?" interrupted Charlotte, taking a gold swatch of silk from the drawer of the sewing table.

"Perfect," exclaimed Mary-Charlotte. "How did you know?"

"It just seemed right," answered Charlotte sheepishly. Of course, she had seen her great-grandmother's patch before, so it felt a little like she was cheating.

"I can't believe you've never done this before. Don't you have a sewing desk at home?"

"No," answered Charlotte.

"Well, then, let me give you something to get you started."

Mary-Charlotte picked up an ornate silver needle case, engraved with Chinese characters. She then placed four needles of various sizes inside and presented it to Charlotte.

"It's so beautiful. What does it say?"

"It's an old proverb. *If you can't make something, at least make a difference.*"

Charlotte placed the silver treasure in the pocket of her robe. "Thank you."

A sudden knock at the door startled both girls.

"Mary-Charlotte?" The woman's voice was respectful but slightly exasperated. "Everyone's headed to the chapel for midnight mass. Please tell me you're dressed."

In wordless agreement, both girls ran to the door of the adjoining room and opened it. A cold breeze greeted them. They both stared into the moonlit darkness for a moment and then, holding hands to double their bravery, hurried inside, closing the door behind them.

The bedroom was like the others the two girls had passed while running through the house, except for one feature: an intricately embroidered quilt lay across the bed.

Bong. The chime of the upstairs grandfather clock reverberated through the house.

A strange feeling, almost like an electric current, moved through Charlotte. She felt drawn to the quilt and walked towards it, pulling Mary-Charlotte along with her.

Bong. The sound seemed to be getting louder.

"Come on," said Mary-Charlotte, pulling against her. "We have to keep going. My lady's maid doesn't give up that easily. She'll find us here for sure."

Bong. It was like the clock was inside the room with them.

Charlotte let go of her hand. "I think I have to go now."

"Yes. We have to go right now," replied Mary-Charlotte impatiently.

"No," said Charlotte, lifting a corner of the

quilt. “I have to go home, and I think this is how I get there.”

“Under the quilt?” said Mary-Charlotte.

“Yes,” answered Charlotte. “I can’t explain it. I don’t understand it myself.” She rushed to Mary-Charlotte and hugged her fiercely.

Bong. The sound vibrated inside Charlotte’s bones.

Mary-Charlotte hugged her back. “OK. You hide under the quilt. I’ll hide in the room across the hall.”

Charlotte wanted to explain, but there wasn’t time. She grabbed the edge of the bed and climbed up, pulling the quilt over her head.

Mary-Charlotte grabbed her arm. “You can’t go under the quilt with that in your hair,” she said, pulling a partially hidden cinnamon stick out of Charlotte’s hair and placing it in her own before quickly leaving the room.

Bong. Charlotte threw the quilt over her head and was immediately wrapped in darkness.

CHAPTER 3

THE COAT WITH THE GIRL INSIDE IT

Underneath the quilt, Charlotte felt a million miles away from the place she had just left. She could still hear a door being opened and the faint footsteps of Mary-Charlotte's lady's maid entering the room. A room that should be just beyond the cottony fabric of the quilt, but that somehow wasn't.

Wherever she was, it wasn't *there*, but neither was it *here*. Charlotte knew that didn't make any sense, but under the quilt felt *in-between* here and there, and she could feel herself being drawn somewhere else, like water inside a straw.

Finding her flashlight, Charlotte crawled slowly towards the centre of the quilt. Soon the familiar patterns of fabric appeared. She turned on her back and traced the patches with her hand. Her great-grandmother's now held a different meaning, as Charlotte recognized fabrics from India, China and Egypt. Some that Mary-Charlotte had collected herself on her travels, others given to her by her uncle. There was even a tiny strip of cloth that made Charlotte smile. It was a piece from her robe, which must have torn off when she fell in the pantry. Her great-grandmother had obviously found it and incorporated it into her patch.

Her fingers continued to explore the contributions of the other women in her family. The patches were all richly detailed, except for one, and Charlotte stopped to examine it further as it stood out from the rest.

It was a simple design cut from a piece of

faded pink cotton surrounded by a large piece of green silk. Both were in the shape of ... people? It was hard to tell. The edges were somewhat ragged in places, and the stitching, by comparison, was very simple. *Whoever had done this wasn't particularly talented*, thought Charlotte. Either that or they were in a terrible rush.

As Charlotte looked closer at the patch of cloth, she began to hear a rhythmic, banging sound in the distance. At first she could barely make it out, but as she tried, the noise got louder, as if the simple act of wanting to hear more details made them clearer. She then began to smell smoke. Again, it was faint at first, but the more she smelled, the more powerful it became. Charlotte coughed as the quilt seemed to fill up with smoke, burning her eyes. She reached out and pulled at the quilt, which surprisingly lifted up and over her head, revealing the world beyond. It was definitely not a bedroom.

Charlotte poked her head out of the quilt, wiping smoky tears from her eyes. Around her were hundreds of people, some sleeping on the floor, others huddled together in small groups. They filled up every inch of space in an impossibly long room with a rounded, tiled ceiling. It seemed to go on forever, and wherever Charlotte looked, she could see more people. Some were angry, some were sad, but all of them had a look Charlotte couldn't place. Men were rolling cigarettes and talking to each other in hushed tones. Babies were crying in their exhausted mothers' arms. Everyone was dirty, and the smell was unbearable. Then suddenly, a loud siren sounded, and people covered their heads. Parents held their children tightly – waiting for something.

The sound of the siren was suddenly replaced by a deafening explosion that shook the room. Charlotte screamed and tumbled off the bed as tiles cracked and dropped from the walls and ceiling, striking some people as they fell. A cloud of dust and plaster then descended, covering everyone. Charlotte thought this was what she must have looked like when the flour fell on her head in the pantry, though this situation was far from comical.

Charlotte sat up, shaken and panicked. She coughed and tried unsuccessfully to wipe the dust from her nose and mouth. She then looked around in desperation and noticed ... something peculiar. Everyone was going back to what they were doing before the explosion. Some rolled over to sleep, others re-lit their cigarettes and continued their conversations as if nothing had happened. It was oddly comforting. In fact, Charlotte realized she was the only one who had screamed – as if nobody else had been surprised by what had happened. It was weird, perhaps not the weirdest thing that had happened to her recently, but weird nonetheless.

Well, that's enough of that, Charlotte said to herself, and she crawled back towards the quilt, quite happy to hop underneath and let this mystery remain unsolved. That is, until she noticed someone sitting nearby leaning against a well-worn mattress. It was a girl about Charlotte's age. She was skeletally thin, with wispy black hair and large sunken eyes. An oversized coat was draped over her shoulders; it was so big Charlotte feared the frail girl might be crushed by the weight of it.

"Are you alright, Miss?" asked a young woman standing over Charlotte. She was wearing a blue dress with a white apron and an odd-looking hat. The apron had a large red cross in the centre. Her eyes were tired, but her smile was bright and cheerful.

"I'm fine," said Charlotte, dusting herself off. She then pointed to the large coat with the girl inside it. "Who's that?"

"Oh, the poor dear," replied the young

woman. "She's been here for three days now. Hasn't spoken a word."

"Where are her parents?" asked Charlotte.

The young woman shook her head sadly.

"Are you hungry?" the young woman asked. Then, before Charlotte could answer, she handed her four madeleines wrapped in a bright blue handkerchief. "Don't tell anyone," she said with a wink. "One of the soldiers is sweet on me and has been saving them from his rations."

"Thank you," said Charlotte.

"Maybe you can get that poor dear to eat something," the young woman said. "She needs food, but I think she needs a friend more."

Charlotte made her way over to the girl. As she got closer, Charlotte could see she was hugging her knees and slowly rocking back and forth.

"Hi. I'm Charlotte. What's your name?"

The girl's eyes were unfocused. She said nothing, her hands clutching a piece of cloth.

Charlotte unwrapped the cookies and offered one. The smell of sugar and lemon seemed to wake the girl from her trance. She looked at

Charlotte. Her eyes were dry but her cheeks were stained from crying – as if she had run out of tears days ago.

"Would you like one?" asked Charlotte.

As an answer, the girl snatched the cookie out of Charlotte's hand. She then turned away and began eating very slowly, like it was the last cookie on earth, and every bite needed to be savoured.

Nearby, an older man in dark grey coveralls began to play a small musical instrument, a little round box with buttons for his fingers. He squeezed it gently and began to play a song that Charlotte recognized instantly.

Silent night, holy night
All is calm, all is bright

Slowly, the people around Charlotte began to sing. Quietly at first, the chorus of voices grew, and the song echoed through the tunnel. The explosion of just a few minutes earlier forgotten. It was the most beautiful thing Charlotte had ever heard. She looked down at the little girl and saw a small smile escape her lips as she wordlessly mouthed the lyrics between tiny bites.

"What's your name?" asked Charlotte again.

"Beatrix," the little girl answered softly. The answer sent a shiver of recognition through Charlotte.

"Beatrix," repeated Charlotte. "From Gladstone Manor?"

Beatrix nodded and clutched the cloth in her hand even more tightly.

"What's that in your hand?" asked Charlotte.

Beatrix uncrumpled the cloth from her hand, revealing a square piece of linen.

"It's my patch for the Christmas quilt,"

replied Beatrix. "Mama said she'd help me finish it when she came back."

"How long ago was that?" asked Charlotte.

"Five sleeps," replied Beatrix. "Sister Lily says to be patient. But it's Christmas Eve."

Sister Lily. Charlotte felt another shiver.

"Maybe I can help you." Charlotte reached out to touch the patch of cloth, but Beatrix pulled away defensively.

"No," said Beatrix.

"I'm sure your mother wouldn't mind," countered Charlotte. "I'll ask Sister Lily for some thread."

Beatrix said nothing and continued to eat her cookie, eyeing Charlotte suspiciously.

Sister Lily was nearby, tending to an older woman who had a gash on her face from a falling ceiling tile. She happily provided Charlotte with some thread and a small pair of scissors, delighted to see that Charlotte had gotten Beatrix to not only eat but talk as well.

"Two victories in one day." Sister Lily beamed, kissing Charlotte on the forehead. "We need more of those around here."

It took some time, but eventually, Beatrix allowed Charlotte to help sew her patch. The little girl had clearly done this before, but her hands were shaking. Charlotte removed a needle from its silver case and threaded it. She then racked her brain to remember what Mary-Charlotte had taught her just hours ago.

"Is this your mother's coat?" Charlotte finally asked, holding the green fabric between her fingers.

"Yes," replied Beatrix.

"We could cut out some of the lining; it's a beautiful green."

"And a piece from my pink dress," added Beatrix. Charlotte saw there'd be plenty of fabric, as the dress was also too big for the little girl.

Together, Charlotte and Beatrix worked on the quilt. Beatrix directing, Charlotte following instructions with her steadier hands. From the green coat, they cut the silhouette of a woman with long hair and a broad skirt. From the hem of Beatrix's pink dress, they cut the silhouette of a young girl. When one was placed on top of the other, it looked like the woman was hugging the young girl. Both were then sewn to the white linen square Beatrix had been holding.

Beatrix looked pleased, and Charlotte was surprised by the results. It looked exactly like the square on her quilt. But of course it would. Charlotte's head hurt to think about it, so she decided not to think about it. Both girls just sat and admired their handiwork.

Beatrix let out a yawn and leaned against Charlotte. Charlotte gave her another sugar cookie, then placed the remaining two in the bright blue handkerchief and tucked it inside Beatrix's coat pocket.

"For later," said Charlotte.

"For later," repeated the little girl, a yawn escaping her lips.

Charlotte sat beside Beatrix until she fell asleep, clutching the completed patch to her chest.

"Sweet dreams, Nana," Charlotte whispered.

Bong! The bell of a distant clock echoed through the tunnel. *Almost midnight.*

Charlotte could feel the familiar pull of the

quilt and carefully walked over to it. Pausing briefly, she looked back to see Sister Lily kneeling beside the sleeping Beatrix, pulling the green coat over her shoulders.

Bong! The bell was getting louder.

Charlotte didn't wait to see what happened next.

She knew how this story ended.

CHAPTER 4

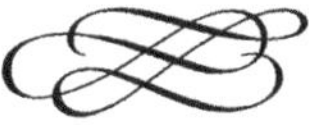

CHRISTMAS ANGEL

Charlotte crawled her way back to the centre of the quilt, the smell of smoke and the sound of bells fading.

She had met her great-grandmother and now her Nana. There was really only one more person to visit, and it scared Charlotte the most. Turning on her back, she looked up at the memories of her ancestors, and her fingers traced the square that belonged to her mother, Margaret.

Margaret's square wasn't hard to find. It was the last one. An intricately embroidered Christmas scene, with a brightly decorated tree, roaring fireplace, and a family of three ... well, actually, two. A mother, a daughter and the faint outline of one other person who towered above them. As Charlotte stared, the embroidery became more vivid, and she could hear – was that shouting? She lifted the quilt, just enough to see.

In front of her was a wall of dark, knotted timber – or rather a *floor* of dark, knotted timber. Charlotte quickly realized the quilt now hung on a wall. She was, in fact, suspended above the floor, yet she did not fall. The effect was dizzying, but remarkably, it was one of the least dizzying things that had happened to her that night.

Charlotte peeked out of the quilt as far as she dared. The room was dim, and Charlotte wondered if improper lighting was a feature of all magical adventures. The chandelier in the hallway begrudgingly shared some of its light, which reflected on the large, worn dining table.

The room was quiet save for muffled sobs coming from underneath the table. Charlotte looked under the table, and was greeted by two eyes, reddened from tears, peering back at her. She recognized her mother's eyes immediately. They may only be ten years old, but eyes don't change.

As they stared at each other, the shouting started again. Charlotte didn't recognize the voices, but she did recognize the words. They were the same words she had heard her own parents use, the words that changed her whole life and the reason there were now two places she and Beatrix spent Christmas. Then the shouting was abruptly cut off by the slamming of a door followed by the start of a car engine. It was all too much for Charlotte, and she pulled herself back inside the quilt.

Lying there, listening to the echoes of an argument long since over, Charlotte thought of her mother. *Mother* the liar, *Mother* the nag, *Mother* who had torn her from her home. A home that didn't require slippers. Except, Charlotte reminded herself, that girl under the table wasn't

Mother. Not yet. That girl under the table was experiencing her own pain, a pain Charlotte understood all too well. Holding the bed sheets tightly, Charlotte turned around and stuck one foot out of the quilt, then the other, and gingerly dropped to the dining hall floor.

Her mother hadn't moved. Whether from shock or fear Charlotte didn't know. "Don't be afraid," she whispered, realizing how ridiculous those words sounded coming from someone who'd just emerged barefoot from an old quilt hanging on the wall.

Margaret said nothing and continued to stare. Charlotte then crawled under the table, carefully navigating a forest of chair legs until they were face-to-face.

They looked so much alike, with big brown eyes and messy brown hair hanging just past their shoulders. Charlotte couldn't remember her mother's hair ever being that long. They could be sisters.

Margaret had built a nest, or perhaps a *fort* was a better way to describe it. She was surrounded by blankets and pillows, books and toys. Everything a ten-year-old could need.

Charlotte reached for her mother's hands. "Everything's going to be OK."

"Who are you?" Margaret asked, grabbing her daughter's hands in a tight grip, making her wince.

Charlotte was about to answer when she noticed Margaret's terrified gaze. It was darting from the quilt to Charlotte to an embroidered piece of cloth sitting at her feet. The patch was exactly as Charlotte remembered, except that instead of a blank outline, a tall man with a big smile stood beside the mother and child. Perhaps the truth wasn't what her mother needed right now.

"I'm your ... Christmas Angel."

Margaret took this news surprisingly well, as if whatever fantasy this strange girl was peddling inside a forest of polished mahogany was better than the reality outside. The look of shock or fear left her face, her fingers unclenched, and feeling returned to Charlotte's hands.

"My Christmas Angel? Like Mummy's stories?"

"Yes," replied Charlotte, realizing at that very moment that it wasn't a lie. "I've come to visit you on Christmas Eve."

Margaret's eyes dropped to her patch. "I thought it was just a silly family story."

"A family's stories can have great power," Charlotte heard herself saying. "They not only tell us where we've come from, but help shape who we will be." Charlotte was surprised how wise she sounded and hoped there was more where that came from.

Margaret picked up her patch and began to

tear at the stitching surrounding her father, which started to separate from the surrounding cloth. Charlotte held her mother's hands again. She stopped and looked at Charlotte, her tear-filled eyes teeming with a thousand questions.

"What's going to happen?"

"I don't know," replied Charlotte honestly. She really didn't know. Her mother never spoke of her grandfather – ever. There were no pictures of him, not even at Nana's house. It was as if he'd been erased from their family. When Charlotte would ask her Nana about him, she would only say that *the winds of fate that push people together can sometimes push them apart.* Charlotte didn't know what that meant when she first heard it, and still didn't know. But she got the impression that her grandfather wasn't a bad man, just a man who made bad decisions – decisions Charlotte's mother never forgave him for.

Charlotte pushed the cotton image of her grandfather back in place with her finger. "What I do know is that destroying your past won't change the future."

"I hate him."

The words stung Charlotte, as she had said something very similar herself not long ago.

"Tell me about him," Charlotte said simply.

"What?"

"Tell me about my grand ... your father."

As it turned out, being a Christmas Angel had certain advantages. One was that Charlotte's mother didn't argue with her. A first to be sure. And as her mother spoke, Charlotte learned a lot about her grandfather. She heard about a father and daughter getting in big trouble with Nana when story time went far, far past someone's bedtime. She learned about them burning pancakes on Mother's Day and having to remake them in a frenzy – their name forever changed to panic-cakes. Charlotte learned many things, but mostly that those memories made her mother smile. An expression she hadn't seen in a long time.

Afterwards, as smiles from past memories faded, Charlotte and her mother held each other tight. They talked and cried and talked some more. They used words that sisters would use to console each other. Charlotte knew what words to say, because those words were the ones she wished her mother had said to her, words she wished she had said to her sister Beatrix.

"Is this a dream?" asked Margaret.

"I don't know. I don't want it to be," replied Charlotte.

Bong. The sound of the grandfather clock sent a familiar shiver through Charlotte. *Was it nearly midnight already?*

"I have to go," said Charlotte.

"Please don't," pleaded Margaret, hugging her daughter even tighter.

Bong. "I don't want to go, but I think even dreams have rules."

Margaret slowly released Charlotte. "Will I see you again?"

"Yes." Charlotte smiled. "And I'm sorry."

Bong.

Margret looked puzzled. "Sorry for what?"

Charlotte gently pushed a stray hair behind her mother's ear. "For everything."

And without another word, Charlotte left the safety of her mother's fort. Stepping lightly on the cold hardwood floor, she was about to climb under the hanging quilt, when her mother grabbed the hem of her robe.

"Wherever you're going, you shouldn't be cold," she whispered, pulling her own knitted slippers off her feet and handing them to Charlotte.

Charlotte knew it was pointless to argue with her mother – at any age. She took the slippers and pulled them on. They were warm and soft and very welcome.

Some things never change.

CHAPTER 5

A GROUP EFFORT

Once again lying in the cozy darkness of the quilt, Charlotte knew there was just one more destination: home. Her stomach told her as much, growling just like one of Mary-Charlotte's tigers on the African plain. *Why do girls on magical adventures never pack snacks?* she thought, realizing that, like Alice, Wendy and Dorothy, she had made the same mistake.

Turning on her flashlight, Charlotte crawled until the familiar patches of family history began appearing above her. She noticed that her mother's patch now had three family members on it, and she smiled at the thought.

Each square was beautiful in its own special way. Mary-Charlotte's, with its silk and satin, Nana's in simple cotton and linen, her mother's with detailed embroidery and ... nothing. There were no more patches – they simply ended.

How do I get home?

Then her heart began to quicken, panic rising as she realized what she had done, or more accurately, *hadn't* done.

I didn't make a patch.

I said maybe later.

I didn't listen to Nana.

I never listen.

I can't go home.

I can't go home. Charlotte felt the full weight of those words. Her arms and legs became heavy; her mouth was suddenly dry. Her stomach churned and she tried to swallow. *I can't go home.* The words repeated endlessly in her mind.

Because there's no home to go to.

Charlotte squeezed her eyes shut. She prayed, she wished, she demanded, but when she finally opened them, nothing had changed. She was still beneath the quilt, a quilt without a patch of her own. She had ignored her past, and now she had no future.

As Charlotte lay there sobbing, a thought occurred to her. It was a tiny thought at first, bobbing in a sea of hopelessness. But it stubbornly persisted.

Opening her eyes, Charlotte reached up and touched that part of her hair where the cinnamon stick had once been. Its scent still lingered, and it reminded Charlotte of something her great-grandmother had said. *If you can't make something, at least make a difference.*

Had she made a difference? Charlotte reached into her pockets and spread the contents out in front of her.

There was Mary-Charlotte's silver needle case, Sister Lily's scissors. *I should have returned those,* Charlotte scolded herself, and a faded blue handkerchief containing half a forgotten madeleine. She then slipped off her mother's knitted slippers. Carefully unravelling them, they provided a good amount of red yarn.

~

As Charlotte stared at the treasures from her recent adventures, that tiny thought blossomed into an idea. She took Sister Lily's scissors and cut a circle from her white cotton nightgown, just slightly larger than her outstretched palm. Then, she folded it in half and then half again. Remembering what she had learned from Nana, she cut out a silhouette of a girl with hands outstretched. When she opened the folded cloth, there were four girls holding hands in an eternal circle.

She removed a large needle from her great-grandmother's silver case and carefully threaded yarn from her mother's slippers through it. Sitting cross-legged, flashlight held between her ear and right shoulder, she then sewed the circle of girls to her Nana's handkerchief, chewing on the remaining cookie as she did.

It wasn't perfect, and Charlotte had pricked her finger three times while making it, but she was pleased. She knew it had been a group effort.

It wasn't perfect, but hopefully it was enough.

Charlotte lifted her patch towards the empty space on the quilt above her head and ... hesitated. Something wasn't quite right. Her square still needed *something*. She bit the side of her bottom lip, which she often did while thinking. *What could it be?* she thought, holding the square in front of her. Then, the edges of her mouth curled up into a knowing smile. She took her great-grandmother's needle and threaded it once more.

Her square complete, she held it up to the empty space on the quilt. She closed her eyes and thought about home – about her grandmother's stories, her sister's pranks and her mother's advice. She thought about cookies on high shelves and presents under trees and hot tea cooling on tables. She thought of frigid floors and warm hearts and laughter.

CHAPTER 6

THE GREATEST PRESENT

Slowly lifting the quilt, Charlotte looked tentatively around the room. It was still dark. She held her breath until her eyes adjusted, and she saw Beatrix's sleeping figure. She was still wrapped in blankets like a tortilla and snoring gently. Charlotte wanted to do nothing more than hug her sister and tell her how much she loved her, so she did. The hug quickly turned into a tackle, and both Charlotte and

Beatrix rolled off the bed. Luckily this was not the first time falling off the bed for Charlotte, and she was able to turn and take the brunt of the impact, her half-awake sister falling on top of her.

"Is it Christmas?" Her sister rubbed the sleepiness from her eyes.

Charlotte put her fingers to her lips and motioned her sister to follow. The two crept out of their room and onto the balcony overlooking the great hall where the early morning sun was just starting to stream through the window. Beatrix squealed when she saw what was under the Christmas tree. She ran down the stairs at a speed Charlotte was pretty sure would rival any Olympian.

But it was who sat around the tree that made Charlotte's heart skip a beat.

They had been speaking in hushed tones, as adults often do when trying to avoid waking sleeping children. There was Nana, sitting in her usual chair, a steaming cup of tea cooling beside her. Next was Mother, smiling so brightly Charlotte almost didn't recognize her. And finally, sitting with her back to Charlotte, was another woman, Christmas tree lights reflecting rainbow hues in her golden hair.

They all turned and looked up as Beatrix squealed, but Charlotte didn't move, too scared *this* might be the dream.

"Mom?" Charlotte's voice cracked.

"Merry Christmas, sweetie," said the blonde woman with rainbows in her hair.

Charlotte bounded down the stairs two at a time, nearly catching Beatrix on the way down.

They sat and talked all morning. They all had so much to say. Nana spoke about the war, Mother told funny stories about her father, whose picture now sat on the mantel behind her. Even Beatrix told silly riddles that stumped everyone except Mom, who was always good at those things. The only one who didn't speak was Charlotte, who just listened. Listened to everything she had been missing.

On Charlotte's tenth Christmas, in a house that no longer seemed as large or as cold as it had once been, she finally understood. Her family wasn't just the greatest present she could ask for; it was also the greatest past and future.

THE END

ACKNOWLEDGEMENTS

They say it takes a village to raise a child. I think the same applies to writers. I know if it wasn't for my village, this story would still just be an idea in a dusty drawer.

Thanks to Mary Ann Blair and Annelise Knoot for their tireless help with editing and for taming my overuse of scene breaks.

To David Shultz and all the members of the Toronto Science Fiction and Fantasy Writers' Meetup. It's been an honour to be part of your group. Your amazing stories and insightful critiques have made me a stronger writer.

Words on a page can evoke images in a reader's mind, but illustrations don't hurt. For that I have to thank the incredibly talented Michelle Simpson for her stunningly whimsical artwork that helped bring this story to life.

And finally, to my family. My wife Kathy, who never tires (well, almost never tires) of hearing new ideas I have for stories. My mother, who has always been my number one fan, and my son, Griffin, who inspired me to start writing, and continues to be my cheerleader and bringer of tea. I couldn't, I wouldn't, be doing this without them.

ABOUT THE AUTHOR

Peter is a writer, filmmaker and podcaster from Toronto, Canada. He began writing children's stories for his son Griffin. When not writing, Peter can be found teaching and performing improv comedy, playing the guitar (badly) and watching far too much TV.

To learn more about the author, and to listen to his podcast, Musings and Other Nonsense, please visit:

www.storiesbypeter.com

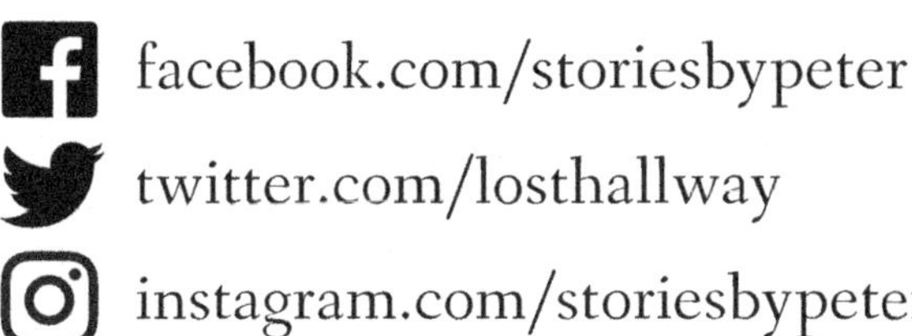

facebook.com/storiesbypeter
twitter.com/losthallway
instagram.com/storiesbypeter

Made in the USA
Monee, IL
25 October 2021